Cotswolds
Travel Guide

Quick Trips Series

No part of this publication may be reproduced, stored in a retrieval system, or transmitted, in any form or by any means without the prior written permission of the publisher, nor be otherwise circulated in any form of binding or cover other than that in which it is published and without similar condition being imposed on the subsequent purchaser. If there are any errors or omissions in copyright acknowledgements the publisher will be pleased to insert the appropriate acknowledgement in any subsequent printing of this publication. Although we have taken all reasonable care in researching this book we make no warranty about the accuracy or completeness of its content and disclaim all liability arising from its use.

Copyright © 2016, Astute Press
All Rights Reserved.

Table of Contents

COTSWOLDS — 6
- CUSTOMS & CULTURE 10
- GEOGRAPHY 12
- WEATHER & BEST TIME TO VISIT 15

SIGHTS & ACTIVITIES: WHAT TO SEE & DO — 16
- BROADWAY TOWER 16
- ST. MARY'S CHURCH 18
- CORINIUM MUSEUM 21
- COTSWOLD WATER PARK 23
- COTSWOLD MOTORING MUSEUM & TOY COLLECTION 25
- COTSWOLD FALCONRY CENTRE 28
- BLENHEIM PALACE 30
- GLOUCESTER CATHEDRAL 32
- CHELTENHAM SPA TOWN 34
- CHIPPING CAMPDEN 37
- NATURE & GARDENS 40

Batsford Aboretum & Wild Garden 40
Birdland – Park & Gardens..40
Clearwell Caves 41
Cotswold Way National Trail..41
Westonbirt – The National Arboretum 41
Thermal Bath Spa 42
Stratford Butterfly Farm 42
Kenilworth Castle & Elizabethan Garden 42

🌐 HISTORICAL CATHEDRALS & CASTLES 43

Berkeley Castle...43
Roman Baths..43
Snowshill Manor & Garden..43
Sudeley Castle 44
Tewkesbury Abbey 44

🌐 MUSEUMS & OTHERS 44

Out of the Hat 44
Nature in Art 45
Keith Harding's World of Mechanical Music 45

BUDGET TIPS   47

🌐 ACCOMMODATION 47

Days Inn Michaelwood..47
The Old Stocks Hotel, Restaurant & Bar...48
Byfield House 48
The Battledown..49
The Ivy House...50

🌐 PLACES TO EAT 51

Piazza Fontana 51
Cutlers Restaurant...52
Lumiere Restaurant...53
Café Mosaic 53
Prithvi Restaurant 54

🌐 SHOPPING 55

Highgrove Gardens..55
Bath Markets..56
Tewkesbury Markets...57
Stroud Markets..57
Cheltenham Markets...58

ENTRY REQUIREMENTS 60

Health Insurance 62
Travelling with pets 63

AIRPORTS, AIRLINES & HUBS..65

Airports...65
Airlines...68
Hubs...70
Sea Ports 70
Eurochannel 72

MONEY MATTERS 72

Currency 72
Banking/ATMs 73
Credit Cards 73
Tourist Tax...74
Claiming back VAT...74
Tipping Policy 75

CONNECTIVITY 76

Mobile Phones 76
Dialling Code..78
Emergency Numbers 78

GENERAL INFORMATION 79

Public Holidays	79
Time Zone	80
Daylight Savings Time	80
School Holidays	80
Trading Hours	81
Driving Policy	82
Drinking Policy	83
Smoking Policy	83
Electricity	84
Food & Drink	84
Events	87
Websites of Interest	91
Travel Apps	91

COTSWOLDS TRAVEL GUIDE

Cotswolds

The 'quintessentially English' Cotswolds is the famous countryside area of southcentral England. This popular tourist destination is close to the cities of Gloucester, Bath, Oxford, and Stratford-upon-Avon. The Cotswolds is an English 'Area of Outstanding Natural Beauty' (AONB) and crosses six counties (Gloucestershire, Oxfordshire, Warwickshire, Wiltshire, Somerset, and Worcestershire).

COTSWOLDS TRAVEL GUIDE

The Cotswolds is the largest of the forty AONBs in England and Wales and is the second largest protected landscape in England (after the Lake District National Park).

The Cotswolds region, famous for its honey-coloured limestone villages, medieval market places, numerous parks and wild gardens, and the beautiful rolling hills in the countryside, has become one of the major tourist attractions in the UK bringing in £1 billion to the local economy. In fact, tourism is the primary source of employment with over 20,000 jobs.

The Cotswolds draws tourists who are looking for a quiet getaway from the hustle and din of city life. The region has numerous walk and cycle trails including National and

COTSWOLDS TRAVEL GUIDE

Regional Walking Routes like the 103-mile Cotswolds Way Trail, and the 146-mile Shakespeare's Way. The hills have numerous vantage points having magnificent views of the countryside. Two very popular points are the Broadway Tower and the Cleeve Hill – the highest point of the Cotswolds at 1083 ft (330m) above sea level.

There is no historic official record of the name Cotswolds, but it is generally believed that it got its name from the 12th century Anglo-Saxon chieftain named Cod who owned the highland or 'wold'. Codswolds over the years became Cotswolds. The region earned its wealth in the medieval ages from wool trade. In fact, so popular was the wool of Cotswolds that there was a 12th century saying - 'In Europe the best wool is English and in England the best wool is Cotswold'.

COTSWOLDS TRAVEL GUIDE

Monasteries and Abbeys used to raise sheep – known as the Cotswolds Lions for their big build and golden fleeces – in the hills. The money they earned was often used to build churches which popularly came to be known as 'wool churches'. In fact, so high was the production of wool, that the monarchy passed Acts to push the use of wool beyond cloth-making and to make sure that the importance of wool remained intact.

The Acts, called the Buried in Wool Acts 1667 & 1668 required all bodies to be buried in wool (or woolen products) only, unless the person died of a natural disease, like plague. The Acts were repealed in 1814. The Cotswolds region is also believed to have been a major Salt Route. Salt was used for dyes as well as medicines, making it an important commodity of trade. Winchcombe was at a crossroads for the salt trade routes that allowed

COTSWOLDS TRAVEL GUIDE

the aristocracy to earn huge sums from the taxes levied. 2 other industries were established in the Cotswolds region but never took off as expected – silk production and tobacco. Silk Lane and Tobacco Close (street) in Winchcombe can still be seen as stark reminders of these failed industries.

Today tourism in Cotswolds has a lot to offer beyond just the magnificent views of its countryside. In fact, tourism is promoted in Cotswolds with the catchphrase – 'The Cotswolds More Than Just A View'. There are a number of popular destinations in the Cotswolds region that include Cheltenham, Cirencester, Stroud, Winchcombe, Tetbury, and Stow-on-the-Wold. Spread across the different regions are numerous villages dating back to the 15th and 16th centuries that have remained almost unchanged over the centuries.

COTSWOLDS TRAVEL GUIDE

Many of the buildings in this region are built with Oolitic Limestone, a natural building material that was found in abundance. The buildings are now 'grade listed' by the UK government, so no structural changes are allowed, thus retaining their original form. There are also many castles, museums, sporting events, festivals, and leisure activities in Cotswolds. The numerous family attractions and low cost options have made Cotswolds an irresistible tourist attraction in the UK.

🌍 Customs & Culture

Whether it's summer or winter, there is always a festival or two listed in the Cotswolds calendar. From comedy to crafts, and from baking to battles, there is a wide variety of festivals and fairs in the different regions of Cotswolds.

COTSWOLDS TRAVEL GUIDE

Theatre lovers can book a show at the Everyman Theatre or Playhouse Theatre, or attend the Open Air Theatre Festival in July at Cheltenham. For the lovers of poetry and literature, there are the Camden Literature Festival and the Cheltenham Poetry Festival during early summer. Music lovers are spoilt for choice, and, quite rightly so. The hills have inspired many British composers and their compositions – Herbert Howells' Piano Quartet in A Minor and Gustav Holst's The Cotswolds, to name a couple. The Cheltenham Folk Festival, Lechlade Music Festival, Winchcombe Festival of Music and Arts, Rhythm and Blues Festival (Gloucester), and Tetbury Music Festival are just a few of the festivals that keep music lovers engaged and enthralled all the year round.

Events like the Olimpick Games at Chipping Campden, the Cheese Rolling at Coopers Hill, the Cliffords Circus,

COTSWOLDS TRAVEL GUIDE

and Football on the River at Bourton-on-the-Water are family attractions for the adults and kids alike. Christmas Markets are the toast-of-the-town in a number of Cotswolds towns in December.

Festivals and fairs are not limited to arts and sports in Cotswolds. The Food and Drink Festivals in Cheltenham and Lechlade, the Garden Party at Gloucester Quays, the Lavender Flower Season, the Hat Festival at Gloucester, or the Cotswold Festival Battle Re-enactment at Stow-on-the-Wold provide the visitors and locals with a wide variety of festivals to choose from.

🌍 Geography

The Cotswolds region is barely 100 miles from London, and less than 50miles from Birmingham and Leeds. Although London is the closest major city with multiple

COTSWOLDS TRAVEL GUIDE

airports (Heathrow – IATA: LHR; Gatwick – IATA: LGW; London City – IATA: LCY; Luton – IATA: LTN; Stansted – IATA: STN), visitors can also choose to fly into the Birmingham Airport (IATA:BHX) or Bristol Airport (IATA:BRS). The London Heathrow Airport is directly connected to the Cotswolds region through coach service run by National Express. Those opting for the train can take a direct connection too; the train goes via London Paddington Station in central London.

Train connections for the 90 minute journey to the Cotswolds region are available from London Paddington Station daily every hour. Ticket costs about £20 if bought a week in advance. Train connections are not available to all the towns in the Cotswolds region; connecting stations are at Oxford, Hanborough, Kingham, Moreton-in-Marsh, Stratford-upon-Avon, Cheltenham, Gloucester, Stroud,

COTSWOLDS TRAVEL GUIDE

Kemble, Chippenham, and Bath. Details of train schedules and fares are available at:

http://www.thetrainline.com/ &

http://www.nationalrail.co.uk/.

The Cotswolds is connected by road through a coach (bus) service run by the National Express - http://www.nationalexpress.com/home.aspx. The coaches start from Victoria Coach Station in London and takes about 3.5 hours to reach the Cotswolds. The coaches stop at many major points including Oxford, Bourton-on-the-Water, Cheltenham, Northleach, Chippenham, Bath, Gloucester, Moreton-in-Marsh, Stow-on-the-Wold, Stratford-upon-Avon, and Stroud. A typical journey booked about a week in advance would cost £17.

COTSWOLDS TRAVEL GUIDE

For those arriving at the train station or airport, taxi service would be needed to get from the terminal to the hotel as the bus service in the Cotswolds region is very infrequent. There are very few connections and buses often ply once in an hour. Taxi service in the various towns of Cotswolds can be found at: http://www.cotswold.gov.uk/nqcontent.cfm?a_id=1041&tt=cotswold.

Once in the Cotswolds region, the best way to move around town is walking. There are a number of walk trails in the hills that provide magnificent views. The region also has a number of cycle paths - http://www.cotswold.gov.uk/nqcontent.cfm?a_id=2626&tt=cotswold. As stated earlier, bus service is infrequent so if one is planning to move from one town to another, it is best to pre-book a taxi or drive. Car hire is available at

COTSWOLDS TRAVEL GUIDE

Bath, Cheltenham, and Oxford costing about £60 per day. (Note: One can even take the 2-hr drive from London taking the M4 or M40 motorway) Although the regular car rentals are available (Avis & Hertz), one can also hire a classic Jaguar for the trip at http://www.classicmotoring.co.uk/. Couples on a romantic getaway can also try driving the famous Romantic Road route - http://www.the-cotswolds.org/top/english/seeanddo/romanticroad/index.php.

Weather & Best Time to Visit

Not only are the hills of Cotswolds very English, so is the weather. A mild climate with occasional rainfall is predominant the whole year. Temperatures touch the high 20s (in Celsius) in the summer with the lows in the low teens. Winters are cooler with the temperature in single

COTSWOLDS TRAVEL GUIDE

digits. Months of lowest rainfall are between April and July. This mild temperate climate attracts tourists all the year round especially during Autumn and Spring.

COTSWOLDS TRAVEL GUIDE

Sights & Activities: What to See & Do

🌐 Broadway Tower

Broadway Village (Near A44 motorway)

Worcestershire

Tel: 01386 852 390

http://www.broadwaytower.co.uk/

Standing 17m high on the Broadway Hill near the village

COTSWOLDS TRAVEL GUIDE

of Broadway in Worcestershire, the Broadway Tower is a folly at 213m above sea level making it the 2nd highest point in the Cotswolds ridge, 2nd only to Cleeve Hill (330m above sea level).

The 'Saxon' Tower is on the 'Cotswolds Way Walk' and provides a spectacular view of the rolling hills of the region. On a clear day, one can see an expanse of 62 miles radius covering 16 counties! The view includes Vales of Evesham and Gloucester, and across the Severn valley up to the Welsh Mountains.

The Broadway Tower, constructed in 1799, is a Gothic folly designed by James Wyatt resembling a mock castle. The building of the Tower was commissioned and sponsored by George William, the 6th Earl of Coventry. It was his wife's – Lady Coventry's – curiosity that led to the

COTSWOLDS TRAVEL GUIDE

building of the tower as she wondered if a beacon on a tower could be seen from her home – the Croome Court – 12 miles away from the Broadway Hill. The beacon could be seen clearly. The Tower, in the later years housed the printing press of Sir Thomas Phillipps, 1st Baronet and a renowned antiquary and book collector. It was also a summer retreat of pre-Raphaelite artist William Morris.

The Tower, which has featured in many TV series and films, including Sherlock Holmes and The Gemini Factor, can be reached through the Cotswolds Way at Fish Hill. One can also go for the steeper climb through the Broadway Village. The Morris Hall in the Tower has exhibitions highlighting the history of the Tower and its surrounding landscape.

COTSWOLDS TRAVEL GUIDE

Tickets to the Tower costs: Adult – £4.80; Child (10 – 14yrs) – £3; Family Ticket (with a maximum of 2 adults) – £13.

The Tower is open daily from 10:00 am – 5:00 pm.

🌐 St. Mary's Church

The Lychgate, Stroud Road

Painswick, Gloucestershire

Tel: 01452 814 795

http://stmaryspainswick.org.uk

Painswick, located in Gloucestershire, is a village and a civil parish (the lowest tier in the government) best known for the Late Baroque (Rococo) gardens and the parish churches. The village with about 8000 inhabitants is often referred to as the Queen of the Cotswolds for its natural

COTSWOLDS TRAVEL GUIDE

beauty. Dominating the skyline of the Painswick village is the St Mary's Painswick, part of the Beacon Benefice in the Church of England. The Church is a Grade I listed building and is believed to have been built in the early 11th century by Ernesi, a rich Anglo-Saxon nobleman.

Over the next few centuries, the Church changed hands from one family to another. Damaged by lightning, fire, and bullet and cannon-shots, it went through many restorations over the centuries. The nave and the pointed perpendicular tower were built in the 15th century. The 17th and 18th centuries saw the addition of a number of galleries in the north and south aisles. Bells were added to the Tower in the 16th century but were replaced in 1731. Today there are 14 bells, most of those from the 18th century that have never been tuned since their installation reflecting the quality of craftsmanship.

COTSWOLDS TRAVEL GUIDE

The highlights of the church are the yew trees and the tombs in its courtyard. By tradition, the Church is said to have exactly 99 yew trees as it is believed that the 100th tree would be uprooted by the devil. (However, interestingly there are 103 yew trees in the courtyard today, and there are 100 yew trees in the plan of the Church leaflet itself.) The 33 tombs of varying shapes and sizes spread across the courtyard, and seem to be guarded by the yew trees. All the tombs are of the wealthy merchants and businessmen of that region except one, tomb number 32, which is of John Bryan, the creator of many of the tombs and altarpieces of the Church.

Tours are available to the top of the Tower. Dress codes are enforced and one has to be reasonably fit to climb the 90 steps and walk round the parapet. Children below 8

COTSWOLDS TRAVEL GUIDE

and individual tours are not allowed; there has to be a group of 5 – 6 people. (Individuals can wait to join another group) There is no entry fee but a donation of £20 for 6 people is taken.

Tours are on Fridays and Saturdays every half hour from 11:30 am – 4:30 pm (and till 1:30 pm on Saturday)

Also See in Painswick: The early 18th century Rococo Gardens

Corinium Museum

Park Street,

Cirencester

Tel: 01285 655 611

http://coriniummuseum.org/

COTSWOLDS TRAVEL GUIDE

Established in 1938, this multi award-winning museum is famous for its Roman collections dating back to the 2nd century. The Museum got its name from the town it is located in – Cirencester – which was Corinium to the Romans. The Museum has a wide collection of Roman artifacts relating to their society and everyday life. There are a few interactive sections including one where a visitor can dress up as a Roman warrior or meet an Anglo-Saxon Princess. 2 of the most important collections of the Museum are the Four Seasons and Hunting Dogs mosaics that were excavated in the mid 19th century. The excavations also triggered an interest in archeological findings in Cirencester that included the basilica excavations in 1897 and the Union Workhouse excavations in 1922. Most of the Roman objects were excavated from the Roman town of Corinium Dobunnorum.

COTSWOLDS TRAVEL GUIDE

The Museum has over 1 million objects and is in a process of listing those online. The collections date from the 2nd century up to the Victorian period in the 19th century. Presently, 60000 objects from the collection can be searched and viewed online. The Museum hosts a variety of exhibitions ranging from handicrafts to paintings and drawings. It also hosts workshops like 'Making a Mask' and 'Roman Saddles'. Evenings are often reserved for film shows (ticket prices separate).

Ticket prices for Museum entry costs: Adult – £5; Child – £2.50

The Corinium Museum is open 10:00 am – 5:00 pm from Mon – Sat, and 2:00 pm – 5:00 pm on Sundays.

COTSWOLDS TRAVEL GUIDE

 Cotswold Water Park

Gloucestershire/Wiltshire

Tel: 01793 752 413 (Cotswold Water Park Trust)

http://www.waterpark.org/

http://www.cotswoldcountrypark.co.uk/

Spread across 40 sq miles in the counties of Wiltshire, Gloucestershire, and West Oxfordshire, the Cotswold Water Park with 150 lakes is the UK's largest marl (calcium carbonate mixed with various amounts of clay and silt) lake system. It has 74 fishing lakes and over 93 miles of walkways and cycling paths. The Park has 6000 years of habitation and is a favourite with bird watchers and nature lovers. So popular are the sightings that one can go to the blogging website - http://cotswoldwaterpark.wordpress.com/ - and list the sighting along with the date. The Park was created with

COTSWOLDS TRAVEL GUIDE

60 years of gravel extraction that were later filled naturally. The Park area encompasses 14 villages with 20000 residents who live and work there.

With numerous water activities like fishing, boating, skiing, swimming, and kayaking, the Park has become a top tourist attraction with half a million visitors every year. One can also try camping, paintballing, shooting, horse riding, rally driving, golf, or cycling in one of its trails. There is also a popular beach that is open Feb – Dec and is the largest inland beach in the UK. Enquiry about the beach can be made at Cotswold Country Park and Beach – Tel: 01285 868 096.

The Water Park is owned by a number of businesses (and individuals) and is managed by the Cotswold Water Park Trust. The Trust was set up in 1996 and aims to deliver on 4 parameters – Access, Conservation, Leisure, and Education. The Trust can be contacted directly for specific queries on the Park at: Cotswold House, Manor Farm, Cirencester GL7 5QF (Email – info@waterpark.org).

The park is open all the year round. There is a £5 entry charge for adults; children enter for free. Activities and food in the Park are managed by different businesses and each has separate individual charges.

Cotswold Motoring Museum & Toy Collection

The Old Mill, Bourton-on-the-Water, Gloucestershire

Tel: 01451 821 255

http://www.cotswoldmotoringmuseum.co.uk/

Founded in 1978 by car enthusiast Mike Cavanagh.

COTSWOLDS TRAVEL GUIDE

The Cotswold Motoring Museum & Toy Collection is a must for car lovers for its exciting collection of automobiles of the 20th century. In 1999, the Museum was taken over by the non-profit organization – Civil Service Motoring Association (CMSA). Housed in a Grade II listed refurbished 18th century watermill by the River Windrush, this 7500 sq ft Museum has 7 showrooms displaying dozens of cars and motorbikes, and a unique toy collection all the year round. The Museum has won a number of awards, notably, 'Museum of the Year 2011' by Classic Car Weekly, Visitor Attraction of the Year 2003 by Heart of England Tourist Board, and the Museums and Heritage Award 2004 for their interpretation project "Big Ideas for Small Children".

COTSWOLDS TRAVEL GUIDE

The collection in the Museum ranges from cars and motorbikes, to caravans and motoring memorabilia. Amongst the notable vintage car collections are the Austin Swallow (1930) and the Morris Minor (1935). The latest car in the Museum is the 1972 Mini Clubman. The motorcycle collection includes a 1920 Indian V Twin, a 1934 Levis, and a 1919 ABC Motorized Scooter. The collection also includes a 1936 Brough Superior – also known as the 'widow maker' for the number of fatalities due to its high speed; the most notable being Laurence of Arabia. The collection also includes children's favourite Brum, television's supercar hero.

The unique motor Toy Collection can transport the elderly to their childhood days with its wide variety of pedal cars and toys. The Austin pedal car or the rocking horse is sure to bring back nostalgia to many. There are also toy

COTSWOLDS TRAVEL GUIDE

boats, model aeroplanes, and bicycles. The Collection not only includes one-off models made by manufacturers but also homemade toys and models.

The Memorabilia Collection includes practical items like brake fluid tins and spark plugs. The Vintage Collection has an interesting mix of exhibits that include vintage clothing, hand-operated pumps, and a set of 1920s art deco racing car teapots.

Entry charges to the Museum are: Adult – £4.75; Child (4 – 16 years) £3.40; Family of maximum 2 adults – £14.95

The Museum is open daily from Feb – Nov between 10:00 am & 6:00 pm. Opening and closing dates of the season are posted on the website.

COTSWOLDS TRAVEL GUIDE

 Cotswold Falconry Centre

Batsford Park, Moreton-in-Marsh

Gloucestershire

Tel: 01386 701 043

http://www.cotswold-falconry.co.uk/

The Cotswold Falconry Centre with its wide variety of birds of prey has become a top tourist attraction of the Cotswolds region attracting over 20000 visitors every year. It was started in 1988 with 150 birds of prey and over the years, about 30 separate new species have been bred in the falconry. Free flight demonstrations are given of some of these birds of prey, and there are a number of tours specific to some of the birds.

The falconry is also a breeding ground for many birds. One can walk in the Owl Woods trail where a natural

COTSWOLDS TRAVEL GUIDE

habitat has been created to make the birds of prey feel as if they are in their natural environment. For the visitors, it is a rare opportunity to watch the natural breeding behaviour of these birds at close proximity.

Displays are held in the summer time at 11:30, 1:30, 3:00, and 4:00pm where the free flying vultures, owls, falcons, caracaras, and eagles soar into the clouds in their own typical style. The Flying Start Tour is a 60 minute guided tour where visitors are given the opportunity to handle different birds of prey. One can also fly a hawk as a part of the tour. Weekday tours are scheduled at 10:30am, 12:30pm, 2:00pm, and 3:30pm. Special Weekend Tour details are posted on the website. The Tour is priced at £40 for 1 person and £60 for 2. The Owl Evening Tour starts at 6:30 in the evening. Visitors get a chance to not only get acquainted with the different kinds of owls in the

COTSWOLDS TRAVEL GUIDE

Centre; they also have the opportunity to handle some of the owls. The Tour costs £45 person and includes hot drinks. The most thrilling and day long tour at the Centre is the Eagle Day Tour. Visitors get to handle a majestic Golden Eagle and then enjoy the thrill of flying an eagle too. The 6.5 hr Tour starts at 10:00am and includes lunch for 2 people. The Tour is priced at £250 for 2 people.

The Falconry Centre is open from Feb – Nov. (Dates for the season are posted on the website) Ticket prices for entry to the Centre are: Adult – £8, Child – £4, Family with maximum 2 adults – £20.

Blenheim Palace

Woodstock, Oxfordshire

Tel: 01993 815 600

http://www.blenheimpalace.com/

COTSWOLDS TRAVEL GUIDE

The Blenheim Palace is the only building in England with the title of palace that did not belong to the Royal family or did not have an Episcopal (pertaining to a Bishop) authority.

The grand country house built in the first quarter of the 18th century was the residence of the dukes of Marlborough. The English Baroque styled building, one of the largest houses in England, has been a World Heritage Site since 1987. It has another claim to fame – it is the birthplace and ancestral home of Sir Winston Churchill and has been home to the Churchill family for 300 years. It is located in Woodstock which is about 8 miles from Oxford.

COTSWOLDS TRAVEL GUIDE

The palace was a gift from Queen Anne to the 1st Duke of Marlborough – John Churchill – for winning the battle of Blenheim in 1704 against the French and the Bavarians. The Palace, built in the English Baroque style, has grand state rooms with stunning craftsmanship. The Palace is surrounded by a 2100-acre parkland and the beautifully maintained Pleasure Gardens and Formal Gardens. There is also beautiful lake in the property. The Estate supports a number of businesses, most notably the Blenheim Palace Natural Mineral Water. There are also a number of leisure and family activities in the Palace grounds including a maze, adventure playground, mini train, and butterfly house.

Combo ticket prices for the Palace, Park & Gardens are: Adult – £22, Child – £12. Ticket prices for only the Park & Gardens are: Adult – £13, Child – £6.50. Concession and

Family Tickets are also available. Note: There is no refund for tickets bought online.

🌐 Gloucester Cathedral

12 College Green, Gloucester

Gloucestershire

Tel: 01452 528 095

http://www.gloucestercathedral.org.uk/

Cathedral Church of St Peter and the Holy and Indivisible Trinity, popularly known as the Gloucester Cathedral was constructed in the last quarter of the 11th century in the northern part of the city of Gloucester. Regarded as one of the most beautiful buildings in Northern Europe, it is a mix of Romanesque, Gothic, and Norman architecture. Located at the heart of the city, the Cathedral is the only location outside London where a monarch was coroneted

COTSWOLDS TRAVEL GUIDE

– Henry III in 1216. The cathedral has stained glass windows with 14th century etchings of golf and (presumed) football – some of the earliest records of these games in the world! Harry Potter fans have seen the insides of the Cathedral a number of times as it was the film location of the Hogwarts School!

The foundation of the Church was laid in 1089 by Abbot Serlo. Over the next 400 years numerous extensions and restorations were done to the Cathedral. Due to the changing architectural style in England during these centuries, the cathedral carries a unique mix of the different styles – the columns are Romanesque, the nave is Norman, and the south porch is Gothic. The Cathedral is 130m long with a Tower rising to 68.6m.

COTSWOLDS TRAVEL GUIDE

Notable attractions in the Gloucester Cathedral include 46 14th-century misericords, canopied shrine of King Edward II of England, and the fan vault cloisters – the oldest in the UK.

🌐 Cheltenham Spa Town

Gloucestershire

http://www.visitcheltenham.com/

Located on the edge of the Cotswolds region, the Cheltenham Spa Town is one of the busiest and most vibrant destinations in Gloucestershire. It is less than 100 miles east of London. Dotted with regency town house with painted facades, the historic Promenade, the popular Racecourse, and host to a number of Festivals, Cheltenham has become a top tourist attraction in the Cotswolds region.

COTSWOLDS TRAVEL GUIDE

Cheltenham is named after the River Chelt. It rose into prominence with the discovery of mineral springs in 1716. In 1788, George III came with the royal family to enjoy the hospitality and the spas of the town for five weeks, giving the local spa businesses a huge boost, and making Cheltenham a destination for the aristocrats. So famous are the spas of Cheltenham that not only the city came to be known as Cheltenham Spa Town, even the railway station is named Cheltenham Spa Station. Historic evidence of the popularity of the spas is found in a 1781 Cheltenham Guide that showcased a visit to the town as 'a journey of health and pleasure'.

Another major feature of Cheltenham is horse racing. The Cheltenham Racecourse - http://www.cheltenham.co.uk/ - at Prestbury Park is a major tourist attraction hosting

COTSWOLDS TRAVEL GUIDE

many major races including the Cheltenham Gold Cup, Champion Hurdle, World Hurdle, and the Cotswold Chase. The main racecourse has 2 courses – the Old and the New Course, as well as a cross-country course.

Cheltenham had a booming spa business for half a century – 1790 to 1840. The period saw a sharp rise in the city's fame and fortune, as well as architectural growth. Although much of it has been destroyed to make way for the new, a walk along the historic Montpelier district still has sparks of the old world charm. The Town Hall, located in the Imperial Square, is an early 20th century building that was built in a Victorian style with Corinthian columns.

The Pittville Pump Room – named after Joseph Pitt, the banker who commissioned its construction – is one of the

COTSWOLDS TRAVEL GUIDE

few buildings from Cheltenham's heydays that have remained intact over the passage of time. Built at a cost of £40000 in 1830, the Pump Room is a popular wedding venue today. Interestingly, the spa water is still available as there is an 80 feet deep pump that pumps the water into a fountain in the main hall. Other famous buildings in the area include the Everyman Theatre, the Municipal offices, and the Playhouse Theatre.

The religious revival of the 18th and 19th centuries were reflected through the many churches that were built in the town during this period – the most notable being the Gloucester Cathedral and the St. Mary's Parish Church (listed separately in this section). The steady flow of pilgrims and followers also gave rise to many small businesses and markets in the area making it a popular

COTSWOLDS TRAVEL GUIDE

market town (see Places to Shop section for list of the markets).

Cheltenham has also become a favourite location for films. Other than the Harry Potter movies that were shot in the Gloucester Cathedral, other notable movies shot in the town include The Remains of the Day (1993), The Whistleblower (1993), Pride and Prejudice (1995), and Vanity Fair (2004). Famous citizens of this region include J K Rowling (authoress), W G Grace (cricketer), Gustav Holst (composer), and Anne Robinson (TV hostess).

Cheltenham can be reached through the M5 motorway. The Cheltenham Spa Express is a passenger train connecting the town with London.

COTSWOLDS TRAVEL GUIDE

🌍 Chipping Campden

http://www.chippingcampdenonline.org/

Located off the A44 and A429 motorways, this picturesque town is in the Cotswolds district of Gloucestershire. The name comes from 'chipping, which, in old English, meant market town. The town is regarded 'a gilded masterpiece of limestone and craftsmanship'. It was one of the most important 'wool towns' of the medieval period and saw its wealth grow manifold during the peak of the wool trade in England. The town was established in the 7th century.

Over the centuries, the city has promoted vernacular architecture, as seen through the typical honey coloured limestone buildings along the famous 14th century High Street. In 1970, High Street and many other parts of the

COTSWOLDS TRAVEL GUIDE

town were designated as conservation area protecting the buildings from any major structural changes. Other notable buildings include the 17th century Market Hall, East Banqueting House, St. James's 'Wool' Church, and the early 17th century Alms House.

Chipping Campden was also a centre for the promotion of local (Cotswolds region) handicrafts with the setting up of the Guild of Handicrafts in 1902. The Guild promotes metalworking, furniture making, and wrought ironwork.

The town has a number of gardens, some of which are major tourist attractions – Hidcote Manor, Snowshill Manor, Ernest Wilson Memorial Garden, and the Batdford Arboretum. Tourist attractions also include the Court Barn Museum, Grevel House, and the Campden House & Gateway.

COTSWOLDS TRAVEL GUIDE

Chipping Campden is chock-a-block with festivals and activities all year round. Popular amongst those are the Music Festival and the Literature Festival featuring artists and participants from even outside England. A popular event in Chipping Campden is the Cotswold Olimpicks dating from 1612, over 280 years before the Olympic Games! It draws athletes and participants from all over England and is a must see if someone is visiting the Cotswolds. The popularity and acceptance of the Olimpicks soared in 1982 after the British Olympic Association recognized it as a part of its pre-history.

Other Tourist attractions in Cotswolds: The British Cotswolds, spread across 6 counties with their numerous medieval towns have several attractions that would take even an avid traveler many weeks to see. Listed below are a few more of the attractions that are highlighted and promoted by Cotswold Tourism.

Nature & Gardens

Batsford Aboretum & Wild Garden

Moreton-in-Marsh

Tel: 01386 701 441

www.batsarb.co.uk

Birdland – Park & Gardens

Rissington Road, Bourton-on-the-Water

Tel: 01451 820 480

www.birdland.co.uk

Clearwell Caves

Near Coleford (1.5 miles south of Coleford town centre)

Tel: 01594 832 535

www.clearwellcaves.com

Cotswold Way National Trail

Fosse Way, Northleach

Between Chipping Campden and Bath

Tel: 01451 862 000

www.nationaltrail.co.uk/cotswold

Westonbirt – The National Arboretum

Forestry Commission

Tetbury

Tel: 01666 880 220

www.forestry.gov.uk/westonbirt

Thermal Bath Spa

Hot Bath Street

Bath

Tel: 0844 888 0844

www.thermaebathspa.com

Stratford Butterfly Farm

Swans Nest Lane

Stratford-upon-Avon

Tel: 01789 299 288

www.butterflyfarm.co.uk

Kenilworth Castle & Elizabethan Garden

Kenilworth (off A46 motorway)

Tel: 01926 852 078

www.english-heritage.org.uk/kenilworth

Historical Cathedrals & Castles

Berkeley Castle

Berkeley (midway between Bristol and Gloucester)

Tel: 01453 810 303

www.berkeley-castle.com

Roman Baths

Abbey Church Yard

Bath

Tel: 01225 477 785

www.romanbaths.co.uk

Snowshill Manor & Garden

Snowshill – near Broadway Village

Tel: 01386 852 410

www.nationaltrust.org.uk/snowshill

Sudeley Castle

Winchcombe – 8 miles northeast of Cheltenham

Tel: 01242 602 308

www.sudeleycastle.co.uk

Tewkesbury Abbey

Church Street

Tewkesbury

Tel: 01684 850 959

www.tewkesburyabbey.org.uk

COTSWOLDS TRAVEL GUIDE

🌐 Museums & Others

Out of the Hat

100 Church Street

Tewkesbury

Tel: 01684 855 040

www.outofthehat.org.uk

Nature in Art

Wallsworth Hall

Twigworth. Gloucester

Tel: 01452 731 422

www.nature-in-art.uk

COTSWOLDS TRAVEL GUIDE

Keith Harding's World of Mechanical Music

High Street

Northleach

Tel: 01451 860 181

www.mechanicalmusic.co.uk

COTSWOLDS TRAVEL GUIDE

Budget Tips

Accommodation

Days Inn Michaelwood

Michaelwood Service Area

M5 J13/14 Dursely

Gloucestershire

http://www.daysinnmichaelwood.co.uk/

Ideal for visitors to the Swindon, Hungerford, and Newbury areas, the 38 guest room Days Inn is ideal for families where children below 12 years stay and eat free.

Berkeley Castle and Cotswold Wildlife Park are nearby attractions. Each en-suite room has free unlimited Wi-Fi, Hypnos beds, and a complimentary hot drinks tray. There is 24hr reception and free parking.

COTSWOLDS TRAVEL GUIDE

Internet room rates start from £56 for Single and Double rooms. There are dedicated smoking rooms.

The Old Stocks Hotel, Restaurant & Bar

The Square Stow on the Hold

Gloucestershire

Tel: 01451 870 014

http://www.oldstockshotel.co.uk/

This B&B Hotel is housed in a Grade II listed 16th century building made with honey coloured stone, typical of the Cotswolds region. It is located close to Stow-on-the-Wold and Bourton-on-the-Waters. The 18 room hotel also has dog friendly garden facing rooms. There are 2 restaurants with full bars.

COTSWOLDS TRAVEL GUIDE

Room rates are dependent on the season and events in the neighborhood. Standard rooms start from £36 and Superior rooms from £46.

Byfield House

Bisley Street

Painswick

Tel: 01452 812 607

http://www.byfieldhouse.com/

The Byfield House is the winner of the 2012 Cotswold Tourism Award for Best B&B. It is a Grade II listed 16th century building with a historic Tudor Hall, and an 18th century Drawing Room. It gives a feel of the old English charm with its medieval oak door, old rugs, and furniture.

COTSWOLDS TRAVEL GUIDE

It is very close to the St Mary's Church and the Rococo Gardens and 6 miles from the Gloucester Cathedral.

Room rates for the Garden Room and the 2nd floor apartments start from £100 for double occupancy. Please note that there is no facility for credit cards. Rooms have a complimentary selection of food and drinks.

The Battledown

125 Hales Road

Cheltenham

Tel: 01242 233 881

http://www.thebattledown.co.uk/

It is a 5min ride by taxi from the station and close to many of the Cheltenham attractions. The Hotel is housed in a beautiful mid 19th century French Colonial villa. The Hotel has a walled garden and free private car park. All the en-suite rooms are equipped with the basic modern facilities. Room rates start £55 for single occupancy and £60 for double occupancy in a Single Room. Breakfast is included in the room rates.

The Ivy House

2 Victoria Road, Cirencester

Tel: 01285 656 626

http://www.ivyhousecotswolds.com/

The Ivy House is in a late 19th century building that is a 3 minute walk from the Cirencester city centre which has the famous Corinium Museum and the Cirencester Park. It is also close to Stratford-upon-Avon, Cheltenham, and Bath.

The en-suite rooms have all the basic facilities. Room rates start from £50 for single occupancy and £70 for double occupancy.

Places to Eat

Piazza Fontana

30 Castle Street

Cirencester

Tel: 01285 643 133

http://piazzafontana.net/

This eatery, as the name suggests, serves Italian cuisine. It has a cozy warm interior and excellent service. Starters of olives and homemade bread start from £3. Pasta and Risotti are priced between £8 – 10. The non-vegetarian main course starts from £13. There is also a wide collection of Italian wines.

COTSWOLDS TRAVEL GUIDE

Cutlers Restaurant

Number Four at Stow Hotel

Fosseway

Stow-on-the-Wold

Tel: 01451 830 297

http://www.hotelnumberfour.co.uk/

The Cutlers Restaurant is in the Number Four at Stow Hotel and serves English cuisine. It is located right in the heart of 'captivating Cotswolds'.

The restaurant has a special menu for Sunday Lunch; a 3-course lunch costs £30. There is a wide variety of meat dishes to try from; specially recommended are the lamb dishes. A 2-course lunch cost £15. The restaurant is open from 8:00am – 10:00am for breakfast; 12noon – 2:00 pm

COTSWOLDS TRAVEL GUIDE

for lunch, and 7:00 pm – 9:00 pm for dinner (closed on Sundays)

Lumiere Restaurant

Clarence Parade

Cheltenham

Tel: 01242 222 200

http://www.lumiere.cc/

Winner of Cotswold Life's Restaurant of the Year 2013 Award, the Lumiere serves British food along with seafood and contemporary cuisine. It is located at the city centre and is ideal for a break between shopping. A 3-course lunch menu costs £28, and a 3-course dinner menu costs £49. There is also a wine menu. Lunch is served 12noon – 1:30pm from Wed – Sat, and dinner is

COTSWOLDS TRAVEL GUIDE

served 7:00 pm – 9:00 pm from Tues – Sat. The restaurant is available for private hire on Sun & Mon.

Café Mosaic

The Woolmarket, Cirencester

http://www.cafemosaic.co.uk/

Sandwiches and baguettes have made Café Mosaic a favorite for a quick bite.

A location close to the tourist attractions and a friendly staff contributes to its popularity. The café does not have any franchises in order to keep a control over the quality of food. Soup of the Day costs £4.50. Paella costs £7.95. Wine and desserts are also served. Special menus are served from 12noon for a couple of hours.

COTSWOLDS TRAVEL GUIDE

Prithvi Restaurant

37 Bath Road

Cheltenham

Tel: 01242 226 229

http://prithvirestaurant.com/

The Indian restaurant has limited seating and it is best to reserve a table. (Note: There is a deposit for seating above 6 people as the biggest table seats up to 8 persons). There is a 5-course set meal costing £35 per person. The 2-course lunch menu costs £12.90. Cuisine is primarily North Indian although there a few dishes from West India. The restaurant has excellent service as it does not book more than one seating per night. There is also a good variety of wine and cocktails.

🌐 Shopping

Highgrove Gardens

Highgrove Estate, Doughton

Tetbury, Gloucestershire

Tel: 0845 521 4342

http://www.highgrovegardens.com;

http://www.highgroveshop.com/

The Highgrove Gardens are the private gardens of the Prince of Wales and the Duchess of Cornwall. Highgrove employs and engages a team of highly skilled crafts people who make unique products for the home and garden. The Highgrove Gardens have regular tours and it is not possible to visit the shop without having booked a tour of the Gardens. (There are standalone stores in Tetbury, Bath, London, and Windsor) Products, which are also available online, include the Coronation Series of teacups (£55), mugs (£25), and side plates (£39). There are soft toys starting from £12. Most of the products are linked with Royalty or Royal events.

Bath Markets

Somerset

Bath, in the western part of the Cotswolds region has slowly gained prominence as a popular shopping destination.

Major shopping areas include the Artisan Quarter (for independent crafts and curio shops), Southgate (high street brands), Upper Town (jewelry and boutique stores, Western Area (local product and produce market along with the Green Park Station Market), Milsom Quarter (designer stores and high-end shopping centre), and Central Area (variety of stores in the historical part of the town). The Guildhall Market has a wide range of products with some specializing in tea and coffee. There is also a Saturday Farmers Market. Milsom Street won 'Britain's Best Fashion Street 2010' at the Google Street View Awards.

Tewkesbury Markets

Spring Gardens Car Park

Oldbury Road

Gloucestershire

Tewkesbury has a very popular town market with 60 – 80 stalls. Market days are Wednesdays and Saturdays. The three main streets of the town – Church Street, High Street, and Barton Street also have a number of shops selling a variety of products. Popular stores in the town include Dough Boys Bakery, Bikes and Bits, and 1471 Delicatessen. Be there before noon to avoid the rush and to find a good parking spot.

Stroud Markets

Gloucestershire

http://shopinstroud.com/

Home to a number of festivals in the Cotswolds region, Stroud is also a favourite for those who are looking for organic products and local produce from the Cotswolds region – bringing it the nickname The Covent Garden of the Cotswolds. Popular amongst those is the Sunday market held on the first Sunday of every month at the Cornhill market Square and the surrounding streets. The Sunday market has a flea market section and food stalls.

Cheltenham Markets

Gloucestershire

Cheltenham was granted permission by Henry III in 1226 to hold a market every Thursday, a tradition that has been carried on for centuries. One can visit the market on High Street and buy a variety of products, from cabbages to CDs. The Farmer's Market held on the 2nd and last Fridays of each month at the Promenade is a place to buy local produce as well as sample the local delicacies. Antique lovers can try the stores at the famed Cheltenham Racecourse; there is an admission fee of £2. The Sunday Undercover market is held in an underground parking place on Chaman Road; it is open from 8:00 am – 1:00 pm.

COTSWOLDS TRAVEL GUIDE

🌍 Entry Requirements

Citizens of the European Union do not need a visa when visiting the UK. Non-EU members from European countries within the European Economic Area (EEA) are also exempt. This includes countries like Iceland, Norway, Liechtenstein and Switzerland. Visitors from Canada, Australia, Japan, Malaysia, Hong Kong SAR, New Zealand, Singapore, South Korea and the USA do not need a visa to visit the UK, provided that their stay does not exceed 6 months. Visitors from Oman, Qatar and the United Arab Emirates may apply for an Electronic Visa Waiver (EVW) via the internet, if their stay in the UK is less than 6 months. You will need a visa to visit the UK, if travelling from India, Jamaica, Cuba, South Africa, Thailand, the People's Republic of China, Saudi Arabia, Zimbabwe, Indonesia, Cambodia, Nigeria, Ghana, Kenya, Egypt, Ethiopia, Vietnam, Turkey, Taiwan, Pakistan, Russia, the Philippines, Iran, Afghanistan and more. If you are in doubt about the status of your country, do inquire with officials of the relevant UK Embassy, who should be able to advise you. Visitors from the EU (European Union) or EEA (European Economic Area) will not require immigration clearance when staying in the Isle of Man, but may require a work permit if they wish to take employment there. If needed, a visa for the Isle of Man may be obtained from the British Embassy or High Commission in your country. Applications can be made via the Internet.

COTSWOLDS TRAVEL GUIDE

If you wish to study in the UK, you will need to qualify for a student visa. There are a number of requirements. First, you have to provide proof of acceptance into an academic institution and available funding for tuition, as well as monthly living costs. A health surcharge of £150 will be levied for access to the National Health Service. Applications can be made online and will be subject to a points based evaluation system.

If you need to visit the UK for professional reasons, there are several different classes of temporary work visas. Charity volunteers, sports professionals and creative individuals can qualify for a stay of up to 12 months, on submission of a certificate of sponsorship. Nationals from Canada, Australia, Japan, Monaco, New Zealand, Hong Kong, Taiwan and the Republic of Korea can also apply for the Youth Mobility Scheme that will allow them to work in the UK for up to two years, if they are between the ages of 18 and 30. Citizens of Commonwealth member countries may qualify for an ancestral visa that will enable them to stay for up to 5 years and apply for an extension.

COTSWOLDS TRAVEL GUIDE

Health Insurance

Visitors from the European Union or EEA (European Economic Area) countries are covered for using the UK's National Health Service, by virtue of a European Health Insurance Card (EHIC). This includes visitors from Switzerland, Liechtenstein, the Canary Islands and Iceland. The card can be applied for free of charge. If you are in doubt about the process, the European Commission has created phone apps for Android, IPhone and Windows to inform European travellers about health matters in various different countries.

Bear in mind that a slightly different agreement is in place for Crown Dependencies, such as the Isle of Man and the Channel Islands. There is a reciprocal agreement between the UK and the Isle of Man with regards to basic healthcare, but this does not include the option of repatriation, which could involve a considerable expense, should facilities such as an Air Ambulance be required. If visiting the UK from the Isle of Man, do check the extent of your health insurance before your departure. A similar reciprocal agreement exists between the UK and the Channel Islands. This covers basic emergency healthcare, but it is recommended that you inquire about travel health insurance if visiting the UK from the Channel Islands.

COTSWOLDS TRAVEL GUIDE

The UK has a reciprocal healthcare agreement with several countries including Australia, New Zealand, Barbados, Gibraltar, the Channel Islands, Montserrat, Romania, Turkey, Switzerland, the British Virgin Islands, the Caicos Islands, Bulgaria, the Falkland Islands and Anguilla, which means that nationals of these countries are covered when visiting the UK. In some cases, only emergency care is exempted from charges. Reciprocal agreements with Armenia, Azerbaijan, Belarus, Georgia, Kazakhstan, Kyrgyzstan, Moldova, Russia, Tajikistan, Turkmenistan, Ukraine and Uzbekistan were terminated at the beginning of 2016 and no longer apply.

Visitors from non European countries without medical insurance will be charged 150 percent of the usual rate, should they need to make use of the National Health Service (NHS). Exemptions exist for a number of categories, including refugees, asylum seekers. Anyone with a British work permit is also covered for health care. Find out the extent of your health cover before leaving home and make arrangements for adequate travel insurance, if you need additional cover.

Travelling with pets

If travelling from another country within the EU, your pet will be able to enter the UK without quarantine, provided that

COTSWOLDS TRAVEL GUIDE

certain entry requirements are met. The animal will need to be microchipped and up to date on rabies vaccinations. This means that the vaccinations should have occurred no later than 21 days before your date of departure. In the case of dogs, treatment against tapeworm must also be undertaken before your departure. You will need to carry an EU pet passport. If travelling from outside the EU, a third-country official veterinary certificate will need to be issued within 10 days of your planned departure. Check with your vet or the UK embassy in your country about specific restrictions or requirements for travel with pets.

In the case of cats travelling from Australia, a statement will need to be issued by the Australian Department of Agriculture to confirm that your pet has not been in contact with carriers of the Hendra virus. If travelling from Malaysia, you will need to carry documentation from a vet that your pet has tested negative for the Nipah virus within 10 days before your departure. There are no restrictions on pet rodents, rabbits, birds, reptilians, fish, amphibians or reptiles, provided that they are brought from another EU country. For pet rabbits and rodents from countries outside the European Union, a four month quarantine period will be required, as well as a rabies import licence. Entry is prohibited for prairie dogs from the USA and squirrels and rodents from sub-Saharan Africa.

COTSWOLDS TRAVEL GUIDE

🌍 Airports, Airlines & Hubs

Airports

London, the capital of England and the UK's most popular tourist destination is served by no less than 6 different airports. Of these, the best known is **Heathrow International Airport (LHR)**, which ranks as the busiest airport in the UK and Europe and sixth busiest in the world. Heathrow is located about 23km to the west of the central part of London. It is utilized by more than 90 airlines and connects to 170 destinations around the world. The second busiest is **Gatwick Airport (LGW)**, which lies 5km north of Crawley and about 47km south of the central part of London. Its single runway is the world's busiest and in particular, it offers connections to the most popular European destinations. From 2013, it offered travellers a free flight connection service, called Gatwick Connect if the service is not available through their individual airlines. **London Luton Airport (LTN)** is located less than 3km from Luton and about 56km north of London's city center. It is the home of EasyJet, the UK's largest airline, but also serves as a base for Monarch, Thomson Airlines and Ryanair. **London Stansted Airport (STN)** is the fourth busiest airport in the UK. Located about 48km northeast of London, it is an important base for Ryanair and also utilized by EasyJet, Thomas Cook Airline and Thomson Airways. **London Southend Airport (SEN)** is

COTSWOLDS TRAVEL GUIDE

located in Essex, about 68km from London's central business area. Once the third busiest airport in London, it still handles air traffic for EasyJet and Flybe. Although **City Airport (LCY)** is the nearest to the city center of London, its facilities are compact and limiting. The short runway means that it is not really equipped to handle large aircraft and the airport is not operational at night either. It is located in the Docklands area, about 6.4km from Canary Wharf and mainly serves business travellers. Despite these restrictions, it is still the 5th busiest airport in London and 13th busiest in Europe.

The UK's third busiest airport is **Manchester International Airport (MAN)**, which is located about 13.9km southwest of Manchester's CBD. **Birmingham Airport (BHX)** is located 10km from Birmingham's CBD and offers connections to domestic as well as international destinations. **Newcastle International Airport (NCL)** is located about 9.3km from Newcastle's city center and offers connections to Tyne and Wear, Northumberland, Cumbria, North Yorkshire and even Scotland. **Leeds/Bradford Airport (LBA)** provides connections to various cities in the Yorkshire area, including Leeds, Bradford, York and Wakefield. **Liverpool International Airport (LPL)**, also known as Liverpool John Lennon Airport, serves the north-western part of England and provides connections to destinations in Germany, France, Poland, the Netherlands, Spain, Greece, Cyprus, the USA, the Canary

COTSWOLDS TRAVEL GUIDE

Islands, Malta, Jersey and the Isle of Man. **Bristol Airport (BRS)** provides international access to the city of Bristol, as well as the counties of Somerset and Gloucestershire. As the 9th busiest airport in the UK, it also serves as a base for budget airlines such as EasyJet and Ryanair. **East Midlands Airport (EMA)** connects travellers to Nottingham.

Edinburgh Airport (EDI) is the busiest in Scotland and one of the busier airports in the UK. Its primary connections are to London, Bristol, Birmingham, Belfast, Amsterdam, Paris, Frankfurt, Dublin and Geneva. Facilities include currency exchange, a pet reception center and tourist information desk. **Glasgow International Airport (GLA)** is the second busiest airport in Scotland and one of the 10 busiest airports of the UK. As a gateway to the western part of Scotland, it also serves as a primary airport for trans-Atlantic connections to Scotland and as a base for budget airlines such as Ryanair, Flybe, EasyJet and Thomas Cook. **Cardiff Airport (CWL)** lies about 19km west of the city center of Cardiff and provides access to Cardiff, as well as the south, mid and western parts of Wales. In particular, it offers domestic connections to Glasgow, Edinburgh, Belfast, Aberdeen and Newcastle. **Belfast International Airport (BFS)** is the gateway to Northern Ireland and welcomes approximately 4 million passengers per year. **Kirkwall Airport (KOI)** was originally built for use by the RAF in 1940, but reverted to civilian aviation from 1948. It is located near the town of

COTSWOLDS TRAVEL GUIDE

Kirkwall and serves as gateway to the Orkney Islands. It is mainly utilized by the regional Flybe service and the Scottish airline, Loganair. The airports at **Guernsey (GCI)** and **Jersey (JER)** offer access to the Channel Islands.

Airlines

British Airways (BA) is the UK's flag carrier airline and was formed around 1972 from the merger of British Overseas Airways Corporation (BOAC) and British European Airways (BEA). It has the largest fleet in the UK and flies to over 160 destinations on 6 different continents. A subsidiary, BA CityFlyer, manages domestic and European connections. British Airways Limited maintains an executive service linking London to New York. The budget airline EasyJet is based at London Luton Airport. In terms of annual passenger statistics, it is Britain's largest airline and Europe's second largest airline after Ryanair. With 19 bases around Europe, it fosters strong connections with Italy, France, Germany and Spain. Thomas Cook Airlines operates as the air travel division of the Thomas Cook group, Britain and the world's oldest travel agent. Thomson Airways is the world's largest charter airline, resulting from a merger between TUI AG and First Choice Holidays. The brand operates scheduled and chartered flights connecting Ireland and the UK with Europe, Africa, Asia and North

COTSWOLDS TRAVEL GUIDE

America. Founded in the 1960s, Monarch Airlines still operates under the original brand identity and maintains bases at Leeds, Birmingham, Gatwick and Manchester. Its primary base is at London Luton Airport. Jet2.com is a budget airline based at Leeds/Bradford, which offers connections to 57 destinations. Virgin Atlantic, the 7th largest airline in the UK, operates mainly from its bases at Heathrow, Gatwick and Manchester Airport.

Flybe is a regional, domestic service which provides connections to UK destinations. Covering the Channel Islands, Flybe is in partnership with Blue Islands, an airline based on the island of Guernsey. Blue Islands offers connections from Guernsey to Jersey, London, Southampton, Bristol, Dundee, Zurich and Geneva. Loganair is a regional Scottish airline which is headquartered at Glasgow International Airport. It provides connections to various destinations in Scotland, including Aberdeen, Edinburgh, Inverness, Norwich and Dundee. Additionally it operates a service to the Shetland Islands, the Orkney Islands and the Western Islands in partnership with Flybe. BMI Regional, also known as British Midland Regional Limited, is based at East Midlands Airport and offers connections to other British destinations such as Aberdeen, Bristol and Newcastle, as well as several cities in Europe.

COTSWOLDS TRAVEL GUIDE

Hubs

Heathrow Airport serves as a primary hub for British Airways. Gatwick Airport serves as a hub for British Airways and EasyJet. EasyJet is based at London Luton Airport, but also maintains a strong presence at London's Stansted Airport and Bristol Airport. Manchester Airport serves as a hub for the regional budget airline Flybe, as does Birmingham Airport. Thompson Airways maintain bases at three of London's airports, namely Gatwick, London Luton and Stansted, as well as Belfast, Birmingham, Bournemouth, Bristol, Cardiff, Doncaster/Sheffield, East Midlands, Edinburgh, Exeter, Glasgow, Leeds/Bradford, Manchester and Newcastle. Jet2.com has bases at Leeds/Bradford, Belfast, East Midlands, Edinburgh, Glasgow, Manchester and Newcastle. Glasgow International Airport serves as the primary hub for the Scottish airline, Loganair, which also has hubs at Edinburgh, Dundee, Aberdeen and Inverness.

Sea Ports

As the nearest English port to the French coast, Dover in Kent has been used to facilitate Channel crossings to the European mainland for centuries. This makes it one of the busiest passenger ports in the world. Annually, 16 million passengers,

COTSWOLDS TRAVEL GUIDE

2.8 million private vehicles and 2.1 million trucks pass through its terminals. Three ferry services to France are based on the Eastern dock, connecting passengers to ports in Calais and Dunkirk. Additionally, the Port of Dover also has a cruise terminal, as well as a marina.

The Port of Southampton is a famous port on the central part of the south coast of the UK. It enjoys a sheltered location thanks to the proximity of the Isle of Wight and a tidal quirk that favours its facilities for bulky freighters as well as large cruise liners. The port serves as a base for several UK cruise operators including Cunard, Celebrity Cruises, P&O Cruises, Princess Cruises and Royal Caribbean. Other tour operators using its terminals include MSC Cruises, Costa Cruises, Crystal Cruises and Fred. Olsen Cruise Lines. Southampton is a popular departure point for various cruises to European cities such as Hamburg, Rotterdam, Amsterdam, Le Havre, Bruges, Barcelona, Lisbon, Genoa and Scandinavia, as well as trans-Atlantic destinations such as Boston, New York and Miami. A short but popular excursion is the two day cruise to Guernsey. Southampton also offers ferry connections to the Isle of Wight and the village of Hythe. The port has four cruise terminals and is well-connected by rail to London and other locations in the UK.

COTSWOLDS TRAVEL GUIDE

Eurochannel

The Eurotunnel (or the Channel Tunnel) was completed in 1994 and connects Folkestone in Kent with Coquelles near Calais. This offers travellers a new option for entering the UK from the European continent. Via the Eurostar rail network, passengers travelling to or from the UK are connected with destinations across Europe, including Paris, Brussels, Frankfurt, Amsterdam and Geneva. On the UK side, it connects to the London St Pancras station. Also known as St Pancras International, this station is one of the UK's primary terminals for the Eurostar service. The Eurotunnel Shuttle conveys private and commercial vehicles through the tunnel and provides easy motorway access on either side.

🌍 Money Matters

Currency

The currency of the UK is the Pound Sterling. Notes are issued in denominations of £5, £10, £20 and £50. Coins are issued in denominations of £2, £1, 50p, 20p, 10p, 5p, 2p and 1p. Regional variants of the pound are issued in Scotland and Northern Ireland, but these are acceptable as legal tender in other parts of the UK as well. The Isles of Jersey, Guernsey and

COTSWOLDS TRAVEL GUIDE

Man issue their own currency, known respectively as the Jersey Pound, the Guernsey Pound and the Manx Pound. However, the Pound Sterling (and its Scottish and Northern Irish variants) can also be used for payment on the Isle of Man, Jersey and Guernsey.

Banking/ATMs

ATM machines, also known locally as cashpoints or a hole in the wall, are well distributed in cities and larger towns across the UK. Most of these should be compatible with your own banking network, and may even be enabled to give instructions in multiple languages. A small fee is charged per transaction. Beware of helpful strangers, tampering and other scams at ATM machines. Banking hours vary according to bank group and location, but you can generally expect trading hours between 9.30am and 4.30pm.

Credit Cards

Credit cards are widely accepted at many businesses in the UK, but you may run into smaller shops, restaurants and pubs that do not offer credit card facilities. Cash is still king in the British pub, although most have adapted to credit card use. For hotel

COTSWOLDS TRAVEL GUIDE

bookings or car rentals, credit cards are essential. Visa and MasterCard are most commonly used. Acceptance of American Express and Diners Club is less widespread. Chip and PIN cards are the norm in the UK. While shops will generally have card facilities that can still accept older magnetic strip or US chip-and-signature cards, you will find that ticket machines and self service vendors are not configured for those types of credit cards.

Tourist Tax

A tourist tax of £1 for London has been under discussion, but to date nothing has been implemented. The areas of Cornwall, Brighton, Edinburgh, Westminster and Birmingham also considered implementing a tourist tax, but eventually rejected the idea.

Claiming back VAT

If you are not from the European Union, you can claim back VAT (or Value Added Tax) paid on your purchases in the UK. The VAT rate in the UK is 20 percent, but to qualify for a refund, certain conditions will have to be met. Firstly, VAT can only be claimed merchants participating in a VAT refund

COTSWOLDS TRAVEL GUIDE

program scheme. If this is indicated, you can ask the retailer for a VAT 407 form. You may need to provide proof of eligibility by producing your passport. Customs authorities at your point of departure from the European Union (this could be the UK or another country) will inspect the completed form as well as your purchased goods. You should receive your refund from a refund booth at the airport or from the refund department of the retailer where you bought the goods.

Tipping Policy

It is customary to tip for taxis, restaurants and in bars where you are served by waiting staff, rather than bartenders. The usual rate is between 10 and 15 percent. Some restaurants will add this automatically to your bill as a service charge, usually at a rate of 12.5 percent. Tipping is not expected in most pubs, although you may offer a small sum (traditionally the price of a half pint), with the words "and have one yourself". Some hotels will also add a service charge of between 10 and 15 percent to your bill. You may leave a tip for room-cleaning staff upon departure. Tip bellboys and porters to express your gratitude for a particular service, such as helping with your luggage or organizing a taxi or booking a tour. Tipping is not expected at fast food, self service or takeaway outlets, but if the food is delivered, do tip the delivery person. You may also tip a tour

COTSWOLDS TRAVEL GUIDE

guide between £2 and £5 per person, or £1 to £2 if part of a family group, especially if the person was attentive, engaging and knowledgeable. In Scotland, most restaurants do not levy a service charge and it is customary to tip between 10 and 15 percent. Tipping in Scottish pubs is not necessary, unless you were served a meal.

Connectivity

Mobile Phones

Like most EU countries, the UK uses the GSM mobile service. This means that visitors from the EU should have no problem using their mobile phones, when visiting the UK. If visiting from the USA, Canada, Japan, India, Brazil or South Korea, you should check with your service provider about compatibility and roaming fees. The US service providers Sprint, Verizon and U.S. Cellular employ the CDMA network, which is not compatible with the UK's phone networks. Even if your phone does use the GSM service, you will still incur extra costs, if using your phone in the UK. For European visitors the rates will vary from 28p per minute for voice calls and 58p per megabyte for data. The alternative option would be to purchase a UK sim card to use during your stay in the UK. It is relatively easy to get a SIM card, though. No proof of identification or

COTSWOLDS TRAVEL GUIDE

address details will be required and the SIM card itself is often free, when combined with a top-up package.

The UK has four mobile networks. They are Vodafone, O2, Three (3) and EE (Everything Everywhere), the latter of which grew from a merger between Orange and T-Mobile. All of these do offer pay-as-you-go packages that are tailor made for visitors. Through EE, you will enjoy access to a fast and efficient 4G network, as well as 3G and 2G coverage. There is a whole range of pay as you go products, which are still part of the Orange brand. These have been named after different animals, each with a different set of rewards. The dolphin package, which includes free internet and free texts will seem ideal to most tech savvy travellers. The canary plan offers free calls, texts and photo messages, while the raccoon offers the lowest call rate. Also through EE, you can choose from three different package deals, starting from as little as £1 and choose whether to favour data or call time.

With the Three packages, you will get a free SIM with the All-in-One package of £10. Your rewards will include a mix of 500Mb data, 3000 texts and 100 minutes calltime. It is valid for 30 days. Through the O2 network, you can get a free SIM card, when you choose from a selection of different top-up packages, priced from £10. As a service provider, O2 also offers users an international SIM card, which will enable you to call and text

COTSWOLDS TRAVEL GUIDE

landline as well as mobile numbers in over 200 countries. With Vodafone, you can choose between a mixed top-up package that adds the reward of data to the benefit of voice calls and data only SIM card offer. The packages start at £10.

Alternately, you could also explore the various offers from a range of virtual suppliers, which include Virgin Mobile, Lebara Mobile, Lycamobile, Post Office Mobile and Vectone Mobile. Virtual Packages are also available through the retailers Tesco and ASDA.

Dialling Code

The international dialling code for the UK is +44.

Emergency Numbers

General Emergency: 999
(The European Union General emergency number of 112 can also be accessed in the UK. Calls will be answered by 999 operators)
National Health Service (NHS): 111
Police (non-emergency): 101

COTSWOLDS TRAVEL GUIDE

MasterCard: 0800 056 0572

Visa: 0800 015 0401

General Information

Public Holidays

1 January: New Year's Day (if New Year's Day falls on a Saturday or Sunday, the 2nd or 3rd of January may also be declared a public holiday).

17 March: St Patrick's Day (Northern Ireland only)

March/April: Good Friday

March/April: Easter Monday

First Monday in May: May Day Bank Holiday

Last Monday in May: Spring Bank Holiday

12 July: Battle of the Boyne/Orangemen's Day (North Ireland only)

First Monday of August: Summer Bank Holiday (Scotland only)

Last Monday of August: Summer Bank Holiday (everywhere in the UK, except Scotland)

30 November: St Andrew's Day (Scotland only)

25 December: Christmas Day

26 December: Boxing Day

COTSWOLDS TRAVEL GUIDE

(if Christmas Day or Boxing Day falls on a Saturday or Sunday, 27 and/or 28 December may also be declared a public holiday)

Time Zone

The UK falls in the Western European Time Zone. This can be calculated as Greenwich Mean Time/Co-ordinated Universal Time (GMT/UTC) 0 in winter and +1 in summer for British Summer Time.

Daylight Savings Time

Clocks are set forward one hour at 01.00am on the last Sunday of March and set back one hour at 02.00am on the last Sunday of October for Daylight Savings Time.

School Holidays

In the UK, school holidays are determined by city or regional authorities. This means that it could vary from town to town, but general guidelines are followed. There are short breaks to coincide with Christmas and Easter, as well as short mid terms for winter (in February), summer (around June) and autumn (in

COTSWOLDS TRAVEL GUIDE

October). A longer summer holiday at the end of the academic year lasts from mid July to the end of August.

Trading Hours

For large shops, trading hours will depend on location. There are outlets for large supermarket chains such as Asda and Tesco that are open round the clock on weekdays or may trade from 6am to 11pm. In England and Wales, the regulations on Sunday trading are set according the size of the shop. While there are no restrictions on shops less than 280 square meters, shops above that size are restricted to 6 hours trading on Sundays and no trading on Christmas or Easter Sunday. Post office trading hours vary according to region and branch. Most post offices are open 7 days a week, but hours may differ according to location.

In Scotland, the trading hours for most shops are from 9am to 5pm, Monday to Saturdays. In larger towns, urban city areas and villages frequented by tourists, many shops will elect to trade on Sundays as well. Some rural shops will however close at 1am on a weekday, which would usually be Wednesday or Thursday. Some shops have introduced late trading hours on Thursdays and longer trading hours may also apply in the summer months and in the run-up to Christmas. On the Scottish

COTSWOLDS TRAVEL GUIDE

islands of Lewis, Harris and North Uist, all shops will be closed on a Sunday.

Driving Policy

In the UK, driving is on the left side of the road. Both front and rear passengers must wear seat belts. If travelling with children, they must be accommodated with an age-appropriate child seat. With rental cars, it is advisable to make prior arrangements for this when you arrange your booking. If stopped by the police, you may be asked for your driver's licence, insurance certificate and MOT certificate, which must be rendered within 7 days. Driving without insurance could result in the confiscation of your vehicle.

In urban and residential areas, the speed limit for all types of vehicles is 48km per hour. On motorways and dual carriageways, cars, motorcycles and motor homes less than 3.05 tonnes are allowed to drive up to 112km per hour. On a single carriageway, this drops to 96km per hour. For motorhomes above 3.05 tonnes and vehicles towing caravans or trailers, the speed limit is 80km for single carriageways and 96km for dual carriageways and motorways. Local speed limits may vary. The alcohol limit for drivers is 35mg per 100ml of breath in England

COTSWOLDS TRAVEL GUIDE

and Wales and 22mg per 100ml of breath in Scotland (or 80mg and 50mg respectively per 100ml of blood).

Drinking Policy

The legal age for buying alcohol in the UK is 18. Young persons of 16 to 17 may drink a single beer, cider or glass of wine in a pub, provided they are in the company of an adult. From the age of 14, persons can enter a pub unaccompanied to enjoy a meal and children are allowed in pubs with their parents until 9pm. For buying alcohol at an off-license, you will need to be over 21 and may be asked to provide identification.

Smoking Policy

In the UK, smoking is prohibited in public buildings, all enclosed spaces and on public transport. Smoking is also prohibited at bus shelters. The law also states that 'no smoking' signage must be displayed clearly within all premises covered by the legislation. The only exceptions are rooms specifically designated as smoking rooms.

COTSWOLDS TRAVEL GUIDE

Electricity

Electricity: 230 volts

Frequency: 50 Hz

The UK's electricity sockets are compatible with the Type G plugs, a plug that features three rectangular pins or prongs, arranged in a triangular shape. They are incompatible with the two pronged Type C plugs commonly used on the European continent, as UK sockets are shuttered and will not open without the insertion of the third "earth" pin. If travelling from the USA, you will need a power converter or transformer to convert the voltage from 230 to 110, to avoid damage to your appliances. The latest models of certain types of camcorders, cell phones and digital cameras are dual-voltage, which means that they were manufactured with a built in converter, but you will have to check with your dealer about that.

Food & Drink

England gave the world one of its favourite breakfast, the Full English, a hearty feast of bacon eggs, sausage, fried mushroom and grilled tomato. In the UK, this signature dish is incomplete without a helping of baked beans. In Scotland, you can expect to see black pudding or Lorne sausage added to the ensemble, while the Welsh often throw in some cockles or Laverbread.

COTSWOLDS TRAVEL GUIDE

For simple, basic meals, you cannot go wrong with traditional pub fare. All round favourites include the beef pie, shepherd's pie, bangers and mash and toasted sandwiches. Fish and chips, served in a rolled up sheet of newsprint, is another firm favourite. For Sunday roast, expect an elaborate spread of roasted meat, roasted potatoes, vegetables and Yorkshire pudding. The national dish of Scotland is, of course, Haggis - sheep's offal which is seasoned and boiled in a sheep's stomach. This dish rises to prominence on Burns Night (25 January), when the birthday of the poet Robert Burns is celebrated. Burns wrote 'Address to a Haggis'. The influence of immigrants to the UK has led to kosher haggis (which is 100 percent free of pork products) and an Indian variant, Haggis pakora, said to have originated from the Sikh community. The synergy of Anglo-Indian cuisine also gave rise to popular dishes such as Chicken Tikka Masala and Kedgeree.

The neighbourhood pub is an integral part of social life in the UK and Britain is known for its dark ale, also referred to as bitter. Currently, the most popular beer in the UK is Carling, a Canadian import which has available in the British Isles since the 1980s. Foster's Lager, the second most popular beer in the UK, is brewed by Scottish & Newcastle, the largest brewery in Britain. For a highly rated local brew, raise a mug of award-winning Fuller's beer. The brewery was established early in the 1800s and produces London Pride, London Porter and Chiswick

COTSWOLDS TRAVEL GUIDE

Bitter, to name just a few. A popular brand from neighbouring Ireland is Guinness. Along with Indian curries, the market share of Indian beer brands like Jaipur or Cobra beer has grown in recent years. Kent has developed as an emergent wine producer.

On the non-alcoholic side, you can hardly beat tea for popularity. The English like to brew it strong and serve it in a warmed china teapot with generous amounts of milk. Tea is served at 11am and 4pm. Afternoon tea is often accompanied with light snacks, such as freshly baked scones or cucumber sandwiches. High tea, served a little later at 6pm, can be regarded as a meal. A mixture of sweet and savoury treats such as cakes, scones, crumpets, cheese or poached egg on toast, cold meats and pickles. The custom of High Tea goes back to the days when dinner was the midday meal. These days, it is often replaced by supper.

Scotland is known for producing some of the world's finest whiskies. Its industry goes back at least 500 years. One of Scotland's best selling single malt whisky is produced by the famous Glenmorangie distillery in the Highlands. Chivas Brothers, who once supplied whisky by royal warrant to Queen Victoria's Scottish household, produce Chivas Regal, one of the best known blended whiskies of Scotland. The Famous Grouse, which is based at Glenturret near the Highlands town of Crieff, produces several excellent examples of blended grain whiskies.

COTSWOLDS TRAVEL GUIDE

Bell's Whisky is one of the top selling whiskies in the UK and Europe. Other well known Scottish whisky brands include Old Pulteney, Glen Elgin, Tamdhu (a Speyside distillery that produces single malt), Balvenie, Bunnahabhain, Macallan, Aberlour, Bowmore, the award-winning Ballantine and Grant's whisky, from a distillery that has been run by the same family for five generations. Another proudly Scottish drink is Drambuie, the first liqueur stocked by the House of Lords. According to legend, its recipe was originally gifted to the MacKinnon clan by Bonnie Prince Charlie.

Events

Sports

Horse racing is often called the sport of kings and has enjoyed the support of the British aristocracy for centuries. Here you can expect to rub shoulders with high society and several races go back to the 1700s. The Cheltenham Festival is usually on or near St Patrick's Day and now comprises a four day event of 27 races. The Grand National takes place in Liverpool in April. With prize money of £1 million, this challenging event is Europe's richest steeplechase. A Scottish equivalent of the Grand National takes place in Ayr in the same month. There is

COTSWOLDS TRAVEL GUIDE

also a Welsh Grand National, which now takes place in the winter at Chepstow. A past winner of Welsh event was none other than the author Dick Francis. Other important horse races are the Guineas at Newmarket (April/May), the Epsom Oaks and the Epsom Derby (first Saturday of June) and the St Leger Stakes, which takes place in Doncaster in September. One of the annual highlights is Royal Ascot week, traditionally attended by the British Royal Family. This takes place in June at Berkshire. There is a strict dress code and access to the Royal Enclosure is limited, especially for first timers. Fortunately, you will be able to view the the arrival of the monarch in a horse drawn carriage with a full royal procession at the start of the day. Another high profile equestrian event is the St Regis International Polo Cup, which takes place in May at Cowdray Park.

Wimbledon, one of the world's top tennis tournaments, takes place in London from last week of June, through to the first half of July. If you are a golfing enthusiast, do not miss the British Open, scheduled for July at Royal Troon in South Ayrshire, Scotland. The event, which has been played since 1860, is the world's oldest golf tournament. A highlight in motorcycle racing is the Manx Grand Prix, which usually takes place in August or September and serves as a great testing ground for future talent. The British Grand Prix takes place at Silverstone in Northamptonshire. A sporting event that occupies a special

COTSWOLDS TRAVEL GUIDE

place in popular culture is the annual boat race that usually takes place in April between the university teams of Oxford and Cambridge. The tradition goes back to 1829 and draws large numbers of spectators to watch from the banks of the Thames. The FA Cup final, which is played at Wembley Stadium in May, is a must for soccer fans. As a sports event, the London Marathon is over 100 years old and draws entries from around the world to claim its prize money of a million pounds. Keen athletes will only have a brief window period of less than a week to submit their entries. Selection is by random ballot. The 42km race takes place in April.

Cultural

If you want to brush shoulders with some of your favourite authors or get the chance to pitch to a British publisher or agent, you dare not miss the London Book Fair. The event takes place in April and includes talks, panel discussions and exhibitions by a large and diverse selection of publishing role players. The London Art Fair happens in January and features discussions, tours and performances. For comic geeks there are several annual events in the UK to look forward to. The CAPTION comic convention in Oxford, which goes back to the early 1990s, is a must if you want to show your support to Britain's

COTSWOLDS TRAVEL GUIDE

small presses. There is a Scottish Comic Con that takes place in the Edinburgh International Conference Center in April and a Welsh Comic Con, also in April, at Wrexham. The MCM London Comic Con happens over the last weekends of May and October, and covers anime, manga, cosplay, gaming and science fiction in general. The UK's calendar of film festivals clearly shows its cultural diversity. The oldest events are the London Film Festival (October) and the Leeds Film Festival (November). There are also large events in Manchester and Cambridge. The high-profile Encounters festival for shorts and animated films takes place each September in Bristol.

History fans can immerse themselves in the thrills and delights of the Glastonbury Medieval Fayre, which takes place in April and includes stalls, jousting and minstrels. The Tewkesbury Medieval Festival takes place in summer and its key event is the re-enactment of the Battle of Tewkesbury.

Edinburgh has an annual International Film Festival that takes place in June. The city also hosts a broader cultural festival that takes place in August. The Edinburgh International Festival is a three week event that features a packed programme of music, theatre, dance and opera, as well as talks and workshops. The Royal Highland show takes place in June and features agricultural events as well as show jumping. If you want to experience the massing of Scottish pipers, one good opportunity is the Braemar Gathering, an event that takes place on the first Saturday in September and is usually attended by the Royal family. Its roots go back 900 years. Over the spring and summer seasons, you can attend numerous Highland Games, which feature Scottish piping, as well as traditional sports such as hammer throw and tug of war. For Scottish folk dancing, attend the Cowal Highland Gathering, which takes place towards the end of August.

Websites of Interest

http://www.visitbritain.com
http://www.myguidebritain.com/
http://wikitravel.org/en/United_Kingdom
http://www.english-heritage.org.uk/
http://www.celticcastles.com/
http://www.tourist-information-uk.com/

Travel Apps

If you are planning to use public transport around the UK, get Journey Pro to help make the best connections.
https://itunes.apple.com/gb/app/journey-pro-london-uk-by-navitime/id388628933

COTSWOLDS TRAVEL GUIDE

The Around Me app will help you to orient, if you are looking for the nearest ATM, gas station or other convenience services.

http://www.aroundmeapp.com/

If you are worried about missing out on a must-see attraction in a particular area, use the National Trust's app to check out the UK's natural and historical treasures.

http://www.nationaltrust.org.uk/features/app-privacy-policy

Printed in Great Britain
by Amazon